...even the promise of freedom

IN THE WORDS OF ABRAHAM LINCOLN

...even the

IN THE WORDS OF ABRAHAM LINCOLN

Dick Yarwood, *Newsday*

promise of freedom

EDITED AND DESIGNED BY A. K. ROCHE

PRENTICE-HALL, INC., ENGLEWOOD CLIFFS, N.J.

For all our friends—

They are too numerous to be now named individually, while there is no one of them who is not too dear to be forgotten or neglected.

A. Lincoln, Esq.
Springfield, Illinois
July 25th, 1837

Except when otherwise indicated, all prints and lithographs in this book are from the Lincoln era, and have been used by permission of The Cooper Hewitt Museum of Design —Smithsonian Institution.

...*even the promise of freedom* IN THE WORDS OF ABRAHAM LINCOLN by A. K. Roche

Library of Congress Catalog Card Number: 79-99965

Printed in the United States of America • J

13-292235-5

Introduction

How far have we come, in a hundred years, along the path to human dignity? The fight for civil liberties still continues. We are still confronted with violence and lawlessness and disorder. We are still disturbed by war and its many facets. We are still confused by the actions of our young people.

This great nation has grown and progressed and prospered since the days of Abraham Lincoln...but have its people really changed?

Four score and seven years ago our fathers brought forth on this continent, a new nation, conceived in liberty, and dedicated to the proposition that all men are created equal.

If A can prove, however conclusively, that he may, of right, enslave B—why may not B snatch the same argument, and prove equally, that he may enslave A?

You say A is white, and B is black. It is color, *then; the lighter, having the right to enslave the darker. Take care. By this rule, you are to be slave to the first man you meet, with a fairer skin than your own.*

You do not mean color *exactly? You mean the whites are* intellectually *the superiors of the blacks, and therefore have the right to enslave them? Take care again. By this rule, you are to be slave to the first man you meet with an intellect superior to your own.*

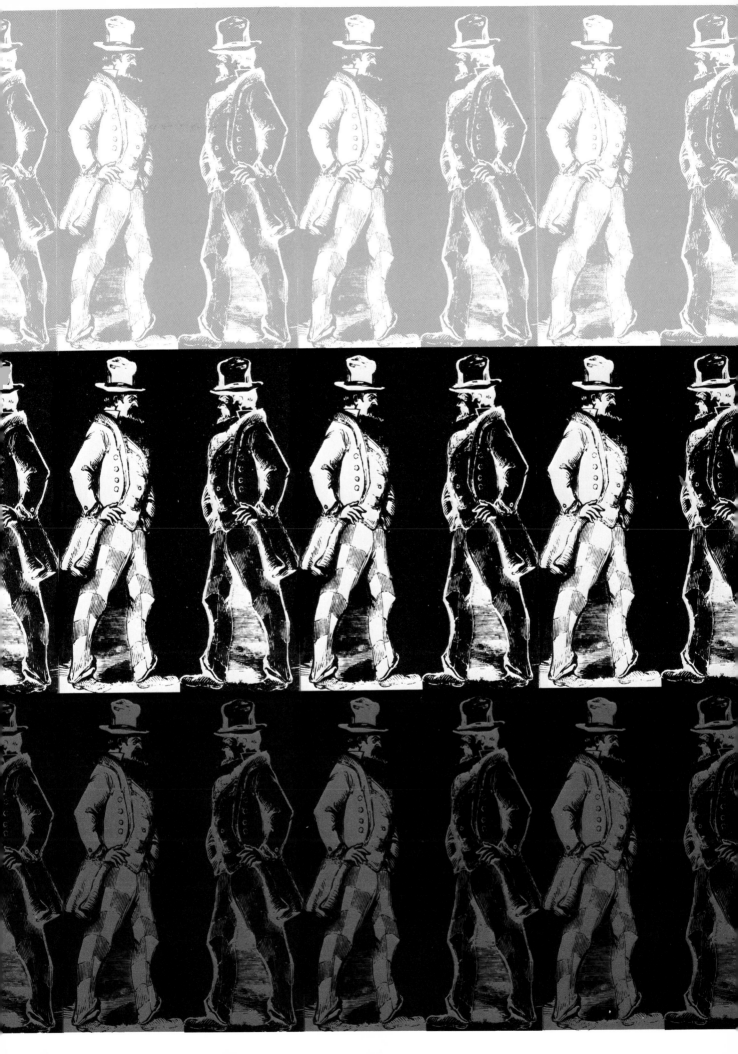

Washington, D.C. rally for religious liberty. *UPI*

Protest against Negro freedom marchers. *UPI*

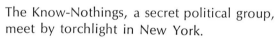

The Know-Nothings, a secret political group, meet by torchlight in New York.

A Know-Nothing demonstration against the Catholics.

*I am not a Know-Nothing
. . . How could I be? How can
anyone who abhors the oppres-
sion of Negroes, be in favor of
degrading classes of white people? Our progress in degeneracy
appears to me to be pretty rapid.
As a nation, we began by declar-
ing that* "all men are created
equal." *We now practically read
it* "all men are created equal, except Negroes." *When the Know-
Nothings get control, it will read*
"all men are created equal except Negroes, and foreigners,
and Catholics."

*When it comes to this I
should prefer emigrating to some
country where they make no pre-
tence of loving liberty — to
Russia, for instance. . . .*

...I protest against that counterfeit logic which concludes that because I do not want a black woman for a slave, *I must necessarily want her for a* wife. *I need not have her for either. I can just leave her alone.*

In our greedy chase to make a profit of the Negro, let us beware, lest we "cancel and tear to pieces" even the white man's charter of freedom.

with certain unalienable Rights,

among Men

The unanimous

IN CONGRESS,

Declaration of the thirteen united

JULY 4, 1776.

that they are endowed by their Creator

States of America.

one people

Laws

When in the Course of human events

Life, Liberty and the pursuit of Happiness—

We hold these truths to be self-evident,

rights,

a decent respect to the opinions of mankind,

that all men are created equal,

…By the fruit the tree is to be known. An evil tree cannot bring forth good fruit.

REJECT
RACISM

LeMay is
OK WE OBEY
our COPS
SO DONT TELL

Violence during race riot in Chattanooga, Tennessee. *UPI*

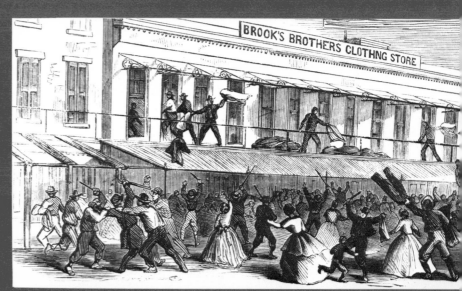

Sacking of Brook's Brothers clothing store in New York City.

Merchandise destroyed during riot.

Looting and vandalism in Cleveland, Ohio. *UPI*

I am opposed to encouraging that lawless and mobocratic spirit . . . which is already abroad in the land; and is spreading with rapid and fearful impetuosity, to the ultimate overthrow of every institution, or even moral principle, in which persons and property have hitherto found security.

The funeral procession of President Abraham Lincoln.

… I hope I am over-wary; but if I am not, there is, even now, something of ill-omen amongst us.

New York, April 25, 1865.

President John F. Kennedy
(1917-1963). *UPI*

Dr. Martin Luther King (1929-1968).
Flip Schulke, *Black Star*

Senator Robert F. Kennedy
(1925- 1968). *UPI*

. . . the innocent, those who have ever set their faces against the violations of law in every shape, alike with the guilty, fall victims to the ravages of mob law.

Lee Harvey Oswald (1939-1963). *UPI*

Selecting draftees by lottery, 1863.

Draft protest, 1965. *UPI*

Draft riot, 1863.

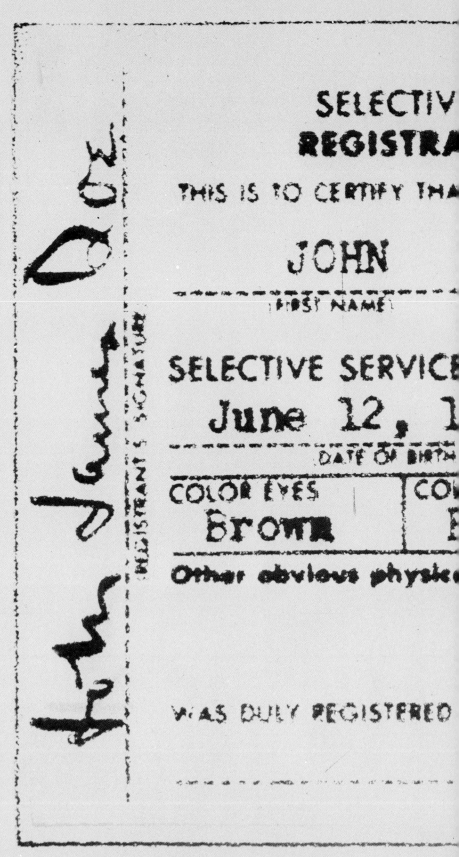

ERVICE SYSTEM
N CERTIFICATE

ACCORDANCE WITH THE SELECTIVE SERVICE LAW

JAMES   DOE

(MIDDLE NAME)   (LAST NAME)

| 00 | 00 | 00 | 00 |

Manhattan, N.Y.

PLACE OF BIRTH

AIR	HEIGHT	WEIGHT
wn	6 ft 1 in	173

racteristics

NONE

14th DAY OF Jan. 19 63

ATURE OF LOCAL BOARD CLERK

15

*The principle of the draft,
which simply is involuntary, or
enforced service, is not new....*

UPI

. . . Negroes, like other people, act upon motives. Why should they do anything for us, if we will do nothing for them? If they stake their lives for us, they must be prompted by the strongest motive . . . even the promise of freedom. And the promise being made, must be kept.

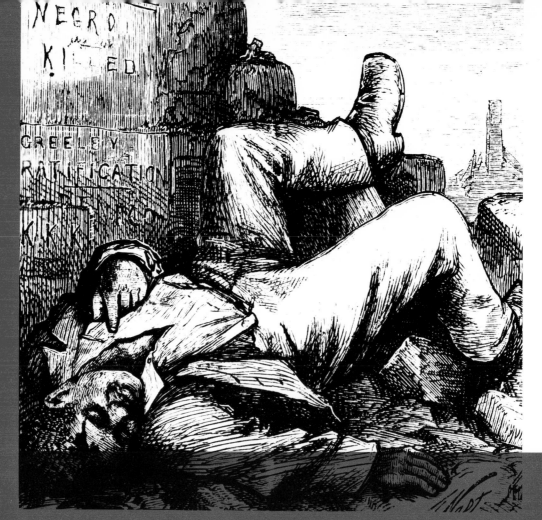

"One Vote Less," a political cartoon by Thomas Nast, c. 1870.

To give the victory to the right, not bloody bullets, but peaceful ballots only, are necessary. Thanks to our good old constitution, and the organization under it, these alone are necessary. It only needs that every right-thinking man shall go to the polls, and without fear or prejudice, vote *as he* thinks.

We have all heard of Young America. He is the most current *youth of the age. Some think him conceited and arrogant; but has he not reason to entertain a rather extensive opinion of himself? Is he not the inventor and owner of the* present, *and sole hope of the* future?

Picture Appendix